Finding Your Sacred Self

Prayers, poems and pastoral helps

Ian M Kilgour

Philip
Garside
Publishing Ltd.

Unless otherwise stated, Bible passages are taken from the New Revised Standard Version, Collins 1989.

Contact Ian at
127 Crossfield Road, Glendowie, Auckland 1071
phone: 027 271 7582
email: kilgours@xtra.co.nz

ISBN 9781991027658
International print-on-demand paperback edition

Other editions:

ISBN 9781991027641
New Zealand paperback edition

ISBN 9798867849337
USA print-on-demand paperback edition 2023

ISBN 9781991027665 PDF eBook
ISBN 9781991027672 ePub / Mobi / Kindle eBook

Philip Garside Publishing Ltd
PO Box 17160
Wellington 6147
New Zealand

books@pgpl.co.nz — www.philipgarsidebooks.com

Front cover photograph:
Spring near the coastal end of the Milford Track,
South Island, Aotearoa New Zealand
by Alexander Garside – Garside Imaging

Contents

Introduction

I have prepared this booklet following a lifetime of pastoral care and visiting with people coping with stress, anxiety and panic attacks. An unstable world, the impacts of rapid change, technology, social media, artificial intelligence, polarised social and political discourse, have all resulted in more mental, emotional and spiritual distress and negative effects on the mental health and well-being of people. More particularly, older people have become very vulnerable to the confusions occasioned by these developments.

Visiting older persons has been one of the great joys of my life. How often I have come away feeling I was the one visited and cared for after listening to their life stories and experiences, in spite of enormous challenges, hardships and sadnesses. We'd often conclude our time together with a scripture reading and prayer, but was this sufficient when the person was struggling with complex issues and needs that required significantly more guidance and help?

One such incident inspired this booklet. While visiting a 91-year-old I shared one of my pastoral helps to assist her to better cope with anxiety. As I explained the exercise her daughter asked if she could write down the suggested steps. At that moment I resolved to write down such exercises so they could be referred to and be more widely available.

It's one thing to know what's needed, which usually the person already knows, but it's quite another matter to share the 'how' of doing what's needed. As we get older it is not always possible to maintain our social involvements or attend church and share in the life of our communities of interest, from which we've received regular help and encouragement. So, somehow, we need to tap into our own inner resources to compensate for this loss. In any event there can be no substitute for being responsible for our own well-being and spiritual life. We all need to develop our own personal ways of how to access and enjoy the relationship with 'divine transcendence' accessed through our knowledge and experience of Jesus Christ.

What follows is a distillation of all I've read over many years. I'm not gifted with much original thinking, so I'm greatly indebted to countless writers, thinkers and poets whose writings I have assimilated on these subjects. I have credited the passages I know the source of. You'll notice some sections are called **'Windows of Insight.'** These contributions, from known authorities or poets, help us to delve deeper into the particular subject.

Ways to use the name 'God'

Readers will note the frequent use of the word 'God.' For those not comfortable or familiar with religious language there are ways to cope with this. The name 'God' means many different things to different people. It has become so general and non-specific that the word can be unhelpful without clarifying what is meant. Many no longer believe in a god called 'God.' To that end the Bible has many names for God while the Koran has 99, illustrating that no one name is sufficient of itself to convey the grandeur and scope of what we mean by 'God.' In the Bible there are many metaphors used to describe God; Father, Judge, Lord, Heavenly King, Mother-hen, Birth-giver, Nurturer, Companion, Helper, Friend, Comforter, Enabler, Holy Spirit etc. Over time other descriptors have emerged which appeal more to non-religious or modern minds such as, Higher Power, Creative Spirit, Wholly Other, Transcendent Mystery, The Numinous,

Divine Presence, Sacred Centre, Universal Spirit, Loving Intelligence, Cosmic Christ, Spirit Presence, etc.

From our childhood we all too easily objectify our understanding of God into a 'superhuman' being made in our image, whereas using other descriptors we can greatly enlarge our understanding. This does not exclude God's Spirit from being deeply personal but is much more than just a 'super-sized' person. As has been said, God is not so much a noun that can be defined but is a verb who actively encourages us to live life to the full. Matilda Mechthild the medieval mystic puts it well,

> God is everywhere and surely, therefore,
> impersonal; and yet in relation to the individual
> soul, God is entirely intimate and surely, therefore,
> personal. She insists, 'that God is for every one of
> us, not in a general, impersonal sense, but there
> (deep within us.) He whispers with His love in the
> narrow confines of the soul.

The word 'God' can also be used symbolically to represent a person's highest values and aspirations. Whatever name or concept you prefer to use, remember all our names and descriptions of God are subject to the limitations of human language and thought.

To this point Jesus urged us to see God as Spirit. He said, *"God is a Spirit: and they that worship him must worship him in spirit and in truth."* (John 4:24). He placed the emphasis on 'Spirit' who is the Presence, actively creating, sustaining, and empowering all of life.

Types of meditation and contemplation

There are many types of meditation. According to Richard Foster,

> they are based on whether we are predominantly using our intellect or our imagination or our intuition. When the intellect is put into operation then the activity is described as **reflective**. When the imagination is employed, the process is **creative**. When we bring into use the intuitive faculty then meditation becomes **contemplative.**

Another group of meditations are described as 'Insight Meditations.' These emphasise **mindfulness, lovingkindness, and concentration.** Each of these types includes many different styles of practice. Suffice to say meditation is a vast field of ways to encounter our true inner self and the Spirit of God. There is no one size fits all. We need to find the practices that best suit us. Note, I use the words meditation and contemplation interchangeably.

Simply put, the aim of meditation is to find God at the centre of our own heart, so our lives can be transformed by that discovery and experience. Meditation is a daily pilgrimage to one's own centre and a way of living from this deep still point of one's inner being.

The practice of meditation and contemplation has a long history and is referenced in the Psalms, Jewish wisdom literature, the New Testament and in countless sacred writings of other religions and faiths. It is said that if we can't find connection with God within ourselves it will make it almost impossible to find God anywhere else! The value of meditation is that instead of prayer being another demand that saps our energy, it becomes the place of replenishment and access to the love which gives life meaning. As Martin Smith has said, 'Our prayer is not making conversation with God. It is joining the conversation that is already going on in God.'

This booklet offers selected ways and means of doing meditation and being contemplative. The first part outlines a recipe for discovering the disciplines and benefits of **'solitude, stillness, silence and simplicity.'**

The second part of the booklet is a selection of prayer and meditation practices, along with simple breathing exercises, that can focus the mind, calm the soul and benefit our bodies. Sometimes called 'Breath Prayers' they have a long history as illustrated by the well-known Jesus Prayer. The benefit of such 'breath prayers' is that you can utter them anywhere and at any time and can compose your own based on favourite scripture, poetry or verse.

Part One

Making space for meditation and contemplation

To create an environment in which we can develop *'solitude, stillness, silence and simplicity'* we need to set aside a regular time and place. Doing this with regularity will ultimately assist us to find that go-to **'sacred space'** within ourselves where we can go and feel comfortable at any time or in any circumstance. To connect with the Divine Presence, using prayer and meditation practices, is literally to make a **'space for God.'** This can best be done by developing the disciplines of solitude, stillness, silence and simplicity which we will explore.

Please note, I'm no authority on such matters. My lack of discipline and concentration, coupled with being too easily distracted by things to do, makes these disciplines very challenging. But, when I have applied myself, I have proved the value of persevering and, occasionally, have encountered transcendent sacred moments of deep and lasting value.

Before commencing a time of meditation, it is appropriate to commence with a brief prayer of your own or the one below...

A 'Prayer of Preparation'

Loving God, I want to come to you at the beginning of my meditation, I want to thank you for this time, place and opportunity to be with you when I can be still and quiet in your presence.

My life often seems so full of noise and activity. There is so much that demands my attention, television, radio, social media, newspapers to read, traffic to negotiate, family matters and people to meet and talk with. Even my own head is full of internal chatter, and I get so easily distracted.

In my work or activities, I am always on the move, bustling and busy, falling into bed exhausted and rising in the morning to rush through another day.

Dear Lord, together and alone with you, help me to meet you in the deep and silent places of my heart. I know that to find you there is to find healing, renewal and peace. I thank You in the name of Jesus Christ who promised to be with us and in us to the end of the world. Amen.

Or as Michael Leunig more succinctly prays:

God help us to live slowly:
To move simply:
To look softly:
To allow emptiness:
To let the heart create for us.

The Way of Solitude

Reflection

Jesus had a need for solitude. Mark 6:31 quotes Jesus as saying, **"Come apart and rest awhile."** It is recorded that one day the disciples gathered around Jesus and reported to him all they had done and taught. There were so many people coming and going Mark complained they hadn't had a chance to eat. Jesus, observing all the activity, said to the twelve **"come with me to a quiet place."** Mark tells us that they went away by themselves to a 'solitary place.' How many times in the gospels did Jesus withdraw to a solitary place? This is the heart of prayer and meditation; that we withdraw each day from the excessive noise and busyness of life to find the life of God in our inner heart and in the 'sacred place' we have set aside. One take on the quote from Jesus is that if we don't find space and solitude *we'll come apart and fray* under the pressures of life. Remember, Jesus said, *"when you pray go into your room and shut the door."* Of course, that room could be anywhere, the garden, a hillside, your very own fig tree, as in the case of Nathaniel (John 1:46-51). Jesus looks for us in our chosen place. Remember his rather sad words to the disciples when he returned from his private prayer in the garden of Gethsemane, *"Could you not keep watch with me even for one hour?"*

We all need to find that place where we can be alone in **solitude** and rest in the presence of God, away from all the demands, duties and distractions of our busy living. The trick of course is to carry this place in our heart so that wherever we are, we'll have this 'go-to-place' available. See Henri Nouwen's comment below about the 'solitude of the heart.'

Luke 5:16 says, referring to Jesus, *"but he himself retired to the desert and prayed there."* In Hosea 2:16, the prophet heard God say, *"I will lead you to the desert and speak to your heart."*

But be warned. Although it can be a place of personal renewal it can also be a place of great testing. Jesus was severely tested in the desert as he struggled against his own conflicting emotions. We too can expect distracting, disturbing images and thoughts to test our resolve.

The principle of first importance is finding a **'sacred place'** where you can enjoy privacy and solitude. You might say, 'but God is everywhere and, in all things,' and that is true, but we are creatures of time, space and place and we need to accept the discipline of finding a place and time and the discipline of going there with regularity, to gain the renewal and refreshment we so need. Doing so measures our degree of intention.

A practice in 'Solitude'

- I see myself rowing offshore to a secluded island.
- I feel the push away from the shore and see all my cares on the mainland receding.
- I feel each rowing stroke helping me to reach the secluded island.
- I sense my feet landing on the island and searching out a peaceful spot (my fig tree) to sit and be, then pause and rest in a sense of calm detachment.

Personal Findings

Jesus saw Nathanael sitting under a fig tree (John 1:48). In scripture, to sit under one's own vine is to find a place of peace, safety, and security.

- Where is my fig tree?
- In seeking solitude what locations do I find most helpful?
- What distractions have I encountered?
- How do I cope with the discipline of regularity?
- What rewards have I experienced?

Windows of Insight

> We don't withdraw from the world to a centre.
> We respond to the world from our centre. Instead
> of rushing about, accepting every job that comes,
> we get a sense of what's really important. Being
> centred allows us to bring that elusive quality of
> focus to our lives. It enables us to set priorities.
> From the centre we can respond to the chaos
> by eliminating that which isn't meaningful and
> bringing order to the rest. For in the centre, we
> are rooted in God's love. In such a place there is no
> need for striving and impatience and dashing about
> seeking approval... Mine was a divided life without
> a nourishing whole. And the disharmony of all
> the competing pieces, the desires and conflicts
> that pulled in every direction within, led to inner
> tensions which had actually become so intense that
> they created physical changes in my body. Chest
> pains and a galloping pulse.

Sue Monk Kid

> The solitude that really counts is the solitude of the
> heart; it is an inner quality or attitude that does not
> depend on physical isolation. On occasion isolation
> is necessary to develop this solitude of heart, but
> it would be sad if we considered this essential
> aspect of the spiritual life as a privilege of monks

and hermits. It seems more important than ever to stress that solitude is one of the human capacities that can exist, be maintained, and developed in the centre of a big city, in the middle of a large crowd and in the context of a very active and productive life. A man or woman who has developed this solitude of heart is no longer pulled apart by the divergent stimuli of the surrounding world but is able to perceive and understand the world from a quiet inner centre.

Henri Nouwen

The sublime and glorious reality which we call God, is to be sought first and foremost in the human heart. If we do not find him there, we will not find him anywhere else. If we do find God within us, we can never lose him again; wherever we turn, we shall see his face.

Meister Eckhart

All this hurrying will soon be over. Only when we tarry do we touch the holy.

Rainer Maria Rilke

Something precious is lost if we rush headlong into the details of life without pausing for a moment to pay homage to the mystery of life and the gift of another day.

Kent Nerburn

When we persevere with the help of a gentle discipline, we slowly come to hear the still, small voice and feel the delicate breeze, and so come to know the presence of love.

Henri Nouwen

O might I 'scape the sordid city air,
This moaning human hive's unresting hum,
Then would my soul, that pinioned is and dumb,
Shake free her wings and all her life declare,
I will away by secret winding stair
To my closed garden whither angels come,
Where the marred spirit,
now unmanned and numb,
May be recovered from her dark despair,
Peace giving healing light for pitiless glare,
Faith bringing vision to the downcast eyes,
Love leaping up the heart's spent treasuries,
Till by God's angels tended and made fair,
I mount again into life's hurrying street,
Strengthened to serve my Lord
with shining feet.

W. G. Braithwaite

In the castle of my soul
there is a little postern gate
Where, when I enter,
I am in the presence of God.
In a moment, in a turning of a thought,
I am where God is.
When I meet God there,
all life gains a new meaning,
Small things become great,
and great things small.
Lowly and despised things
are shot through with glory.
My troubles seem but the pebbles on the road,
My joys seem like everlasting hills,
All my fever is gone in the great peace of God,
And I pass through the door
from Time into Eternity.

Walter Rauschenbusch

The Way of Stillness

Reflection

The essence of meditation is our longing and need for God, waiting on God, listening to God, opening to God. Doing so we find, *"The kingdom of God is within you"* as Jesus said. We've also heard the famous words of St Augustine, *"You have made us for yourself O Lord, and our hearts are restless until they rest in thee."*

To be physically **still** is very difficult. We are so active with so many tasks and duties to perform we can get physically exhausted just trying to keep up with the pace of everything. However, it is even more difficult to quieten and still the mind and heart. When we seek to be still, we find our minds still racing, a lot of head chatter going on and our hearts are restless, often possessed by our conflicting emotions. God of course is still with us in all such distraction but to hear God's personal word to us we must pause, be still and listen, *"He leads me beside the still waters, He restores my soul,"* (Psalm 23). *"Then Samuel said, 'Speak, for your servant is listening.'"* (1 Samuel 3:1-21).

A practice in 'Stillness'

Imagine dropping a pebble into a pool and seeing it sink through various levels while on the surface there are ever-widening circles.

- See the pebble dropping through the surface of debris, chatter, distractions, pains, pleasures, anxieties we hold in our minds and hearts.
- Dropping through our arguments, analysis, rationalisations, and limited understandings.

- Dropping through the layer of our senses, seeing, feeling, knowing.
- See the pebble arriving at the 'still point' or 'sacred self,' where all is 'Being.'
- I see myself in the field of God's spaciousness and grace – where all things are possible – 'Self-Actualisation' as Abraham Maslow describes it.
- I visualise the ever-widening circles of effect that my meditation has on the surface of my personal life and beyond to others and the world.

Personal Findings

- What helps me achieve stillness?
- What areas of my life are hardest to still?
- What changes can I make to change this?
- Did I arrive at the 'still point' deep within me?
- What are the benefits of stillness I've experienced?

Windows of Insight

Unless there is a still-centre in the middle of the storm. Unless a person in the midst of all their activities preserves a secret room in their heart where they stand alone before God, unless we do this, we will lose all sense of spiritual direction and become fragmented and distracted.

Michael Ramsey

In the stillness of the quiet, if we listen, we can hear the whisper in the heart giving strength to weakness, courage to fear, hope to despair.

Howard Thurman

The Daoists (early Chinese religious philosophers) had developed a form of contemplation called 'quiet sitting,' which emptied the mind of preconceived ideas and made it more receptive to outside influences.

Karen Armstrong

To meet everything and everyone through stillness instead of mental noise is the greatest gift you can offer to the universe.

Eckhart Tolle

We find our quiet minds as we sit still with our breath, as we make small jottings in our books, and as we practise silent waiting. Then one day, 'the little ways' open into broad expanses.

Marv & Nancy Hiles

Let us, then, labour for an inward stillness –
An inward stillness and an inward healing.
That perfect silence where the lips and heart
Are still, and we no longer entertain,
Our own imperfect thoughts and vain opinions,
But God alone speaks in us, and we wait
In singleness of heart, that we may know
His will, and in silence of our spirits,
That we may do his will and do that only.

Henry Wadsworth Longfellow

Deep and silent and cool as a brood,
still tree-shaded river
Is the peace of your presence
and the rest of our souls.
From the thousand problems
of this our hurrying life
We turn, with silent joy, to plunge in you,

To steep our souls in your quiet depths
Where no clamour of earth
disturbs our perfect content.
You are our home and refuge;
In you we are safe and at peace:
Even in the din and hurry of the world
We know that you are near,
We know that close at hand
– closer than our little life –
floweth that silent river
of your presence and love.
In a moment we may be with you and in you,
In a moment be surrounded
and soaked in your peace:
In a moment, as this loud world clangs round us,
We may rest secure in this bliss of your eternity.

John S Hoyland

O Sabbath rest by Galilee! O calm of hills above,
Where Jesus knelt to share with thee,
The silence of eternity, Interpreted by love!

Drop thy still dews of quietness,
Till all our strivings cease;
Take from our souls the strain and stress,
And let our ordered lives confess,
The beauty of thy peace.

John Greenleaf Whittier

The Way of Silence

Reflection

In Luke 17:20-21 Jesus says,

> The kingdom of God does not come in such a way
> as to be seen. No one will say 'look here it is', or
> 'there it is' because the kingdom of God is within
> you.

Jesus emphasised quiet prayer in our own 'inner room' and told us not to, "*babble on as the pagans do.*" (Matthew 6:5-7).

Thomas Merton said,

> The highest form of prayer is not a prayer for
> anything. It is a deep profound silence, in which
> we allow ourselves to be still and know our God. In
> that silence we are changed, we are calmed, we are
> illumined.

Each Christmas the well known Christmas Carol moves our hearts, "*How silently, how silently, The wondrous gift is given! So, God imparts to human hearts, The blessing of his heaven. No ear may hear his coming, but in this world of sin, Where meek souls will receive Him still, The dear Christ enters in.*"

Red Rogers said, "*Our society is much more interested in information than wonder, in noise rather than silence. And I feel that we need a lot more wonder and a lot more silence in our lives.*" If we let the mystery, beauty and wonder sit deeply in our silence, our hearts will burst with thanksgiving and gratitude to life itself.

We often fear **silence** because in those moments we have to face who we really are. Somehow silence makes us feel uneasy and so we fill the silent gaps with noise or superficial talk. But if we persevere and drill down into **'deep silence'** we can find our true self and know ourselves deeply loved by God. As God said to Hosea, *"I will lead you into the desert and speak to your heart."* Approaching the Cross Jesus also needed times of silence in the garden where he could commune with God and have confirmed that he was doing the will of his Father God. It is said the language of God is 'silence interpreted by love!'

A practice in 'silence'

- As a thought comes into my mind, I identify it and then just as quickly discard it.
- Keep doing this until there are no recurring thoughts.
- Once my mind is empty, I dwell in the 'silence interpreted by love.'
- Repeat: *"Silently now I wait for You, ready my God Your will to see, open my eyes illumine me, Spirit Divine."*

Personal Findings

- Was I able to shut down my mind's inner chatter?
- Did I achieve at least a momentary time of inner silence?
- Did I realise in those 'silent moments' a new quality of time and being?
- I resolve to persevere and lengthen those 'silent moments.'

Windows of Insight

Meditation is a way of coming to your own centre, coming to the foundation of your own being, and remaining there – still, silent, attentive. Meditation is in essence a way of learning to become awake, to be fully alive and be still. The way to that wakefulness is silence and stillness. ...The purpose

of meditation and the challenge of meditation
is to allow ourselves to become silent enough to
allow this interior silence to emerge. Silence is the
language of the spirit... the all-important aim in
Christian meditation is to allow God's mysterious
and silent presence within us to become more
and more not only a reality, but the reality in our
lives; to let it become that reality which gives
meaning, shape and purpose to everything we do,
to everything we are.

John Main

In the 'marketplace' we meet God incarnate,
God made humankind. God made you, God
made neighbours, made needy strangers. In the
'marketplace' we meet God socially. But the desert
is much more personal. The essence of the desert
is that we are alone with God. It is the place of
personal encounter. This can be very scary yet
wonderfully rewarding. It can be a creative silence
in which we hear God's still, small voice and come
to discern God's will. The desert is so often the
place of personal spiritual experience because, like
for the Hebrews, it is a place of testing, the place
of no home, no cities, no comforts or riches, no
possessions, just the necessities. We are as we are!

Henri Nouwen

Silence enables us to be aware of God ... to let
mind and imagination dwell upon his truth... to
let prayer be listening before it is talking ... and to
discover our own selves. There comes sometimes
an interior silence in which the soul discovers
itself in a new dimension of energy and peace, a
dimension which the restless life can miss.

Michael Ramsey

We forget that in the silence of the heart God
speaks, and from the fullness of the heart we speak.
Only when we have heard him in the silence of our
hearts, only when we have learned to listen to God
in the silence of our hearts, only then can we say: I
pray. There is no either/or about prayer and love.
We can't say we have either prayer or love: There is
no prayer without love and no love without prayer.

> The fruit of silence is prayer.
> The fruit of prayer is faith.
> The fruit of faith is love.
> The fruit of love is service.
> The fruit of service is peace.
>
> *Mother Teressa*

The trees, the flowers, the plants grow in silence.
The stars, the sun, the moon move in silence.
Silence gives us a new perspective.

Mother Teresa

Within us is the soul of the whole, the wise silence,
the universal beauty, the eternal One.

Ralph Waldo Emerson

Life's meaning is found in one way or another
in making connection with the source of life,
mysterious though it is. We can begin to make
this connection by becoming aware of the deepest
feelings and intuitions within ourselves, below the
level of words – silence therefore is a deliberate
and necessary discipline in the spiritual quest.

Rex Ambler

Silence is a kind of wholeness. It can absorb contraries. It can absorb paradoxes and contradictions. Maybe that is why we do not like silence. There is nothing to argue about in true inner silence, and the mind likes to argue. It gives us something to do.

Richard Rohr

Endless invention, endless experiment,
Brings knowledge of motion, but not of stillness;
Knowledge of speech, but not of silence;
Knowledge of words, and ignorance of the Word
...
Where is the life we have lost in the living?
Where is the wisdom we have lost in knowledge?
Where is the knowledge we have lost in
information.

T.S. Elliot

O God, let me rise to the edges of time
and open my life to your eternity.
Let me run to the edges of space
and gaze at your immensity.
Let me climb through the barriers of sound
and pass into your silence,
And then, in stillness and silence
let me adore you,
Who are Life – Light – Love –
without beginning and without end,
The Source – the Sustainer – the Restorer –
the Purifier – of all that is.
The Love who has bound earth to heaven
by the beams of a cross.
The Healer who has renewed a dying race
by the blood of a chalice.

The God who has taken humankind into your
glory by the wounds of sacrifice.
God ... God ... God ... Blessed be God.
Let me adore you. Amen

John Nicholas Grou

Mid all the traffic of the ways,
turmoil's without, within,
Make in my heart a quiet place,
and come and dwell therein.
A little shine of quietness, all sacred to Thyself,
where thou shalt all my soul possess,
and I may find myself.
Come, occupy my silent place,
and make Thy dwelling there
More grace is wrought in quietness
than any is aware.

John Oxenham

The Way of Simplicity

Reflection

Meditation, as one T-Shirt put it, is 'not what you think.' *The Cloud of Unknowing* says, *"He may well be loved, but he may never be thought. He may be reached and held close by means of love, but never by means of thought."* Meditation teaches us that 'being' is more important than 'doing.' The heart is more important than the mind. Our role is to be content with a loving, peaceful openness to God, without concern, without the desire to taste, or cling to, or possess God. We simply listen, watch and wait even though nothing seems to happen. In the Garden of Gethsemane Jesus says to his disciples, *"could you not watch one hour with me?"* In our daily periods of meditation, we watch with Jesus. In meditation we simply surrender ourselves and rest in God.

Meditation is built on a simple premise, namely that our finite minds cannot grasp the infinity of God. However, when words, images and ideas are abandoned in silence we can come to an intuitive knowledge and love of God. Meditation is seeking God in the stillness beyond words or thoughts. Life in many ways seems so complicated largely because we make it that way. It becomes a reflection of our complex personalities and temperaments which in turn can make our relationships complicated. We can also spill this into our Christian life where we can complicate our faith by trying to live according to rules, bygone traditions and by having the right beliefs about God. Theology is always trying to understand the meaning of God with the mind and then organising the Church into systems of belief and practice that we adopt and think everybody else should live by. Jesus, however, spoke more about having a heart faith and trust in simple but lasting values. Jesus was crucified because he challenged the system of laws and rituals as practised and enforced by the religious of his day. It's not about a complicated religion which burdens ordinary people. Rather He dared to simplify life by demonstrating that life is about journeying together in our common humanity, *"loving God and our neighbours, as we love ourselves," and* serving the needs and common good of our communities in direct and simple ways.

A practice in 'Simplicity'

- I visualise my favourite flower or lily, (Matthew 6:28-31)
- I expand my vision to see all such flowers or lilies growing in the fields.
- I reflect on the fact that they neither sow nor reap yet grow in beauty.
- They just are, just as I am, and so I can be just myself.

Personal Findings

- What ways can I simplify my life?
- How can I appreciate my own inner beauty?
- Do I need to declutter my mind and find a new clear focus?
- What are the benefits if I 'simplify?'

Windows of Insight

Praying
It doesn't have to be
the blue iris, it could be
weeds in a vacant lot, or a few
small stones.

just pay attention, then patch
a few words together and don't try to make
them elaborate,

this isn't a contest but the doorway
into thanks, and a silence in which another voice
may speak.

Mary Oliver

Meditation is not a time for words, however beautifully and sincerely phrased. All our words are wholly ineffective when we come to enter into this deep and mysterious communion with God. In order to come into this holy and mysterious communion with the word of God indwelling within us, we must first have the courage to become more and more silent. In a deep, creative silence, we meet God in a way which transcends all our powers of intellect and language. We have to listen, to concentrate, to attend rather than to think. Silence is really absolutely necessary for the human spirit if it is really to thrive, and not only just to thrive, but to be creative, to have a creative response to life, to our environment, to friends. Because the silence gives our spirit room to breathe, room to be. In silence, you don't have to be justifying yourself, apologising for yourself, trying to impress anyone. You just have to be, and it's a most marvellous experience when you come to it.

And the wonder of it is in that experience, you are completely free. You are not trying to play any role; you are not trying to fulfil anyone's expectation.

John Main

In meditation we go beyond thoughts, words, images into a deeper state of consciousness; we call this silence, a place where the Spirit actively works within us when the mind, senses and emotions have been quieted. The inner stillness and attentive listening in this silence is a total surrender to God in the depths of our being. Silence is the door that opens to the kingdom of God within. But we need to be reminded that the silence of the heart is always a gift, a grace which cannot be won through exertion or will power on our part. You discover in the silence that you are loved, that you are lovable. It is the discovery everyone must make in their lives if they are going to become fully themselves and fully human."

Paul Harris

Your vision will become clear only when you can look into your heart. Who looks outside, dreams, who looks inside, awakes.

Carl Gustav Jung

Prayers are tools not for doing or getting, but for being and becoming.

Eugene Peterson

People are like stained glass windows: They sparkle and shine when the sun is out, but when the darkness sets in, their true beauty is revealed only if there is a light within.

Elisabeth Kubler-Ross

I, who live by words, am wordless
when I try my words in prayer.
All language turns to silence.
Prayer will take my words
and then reveal their emptiness.
The stilled voice learns to hold its peace,
to listen with the heart,
to silence that is joy – is adoration.
The self is shattered, all words torn apart.
In this strange, patterned time
of contemplation, that, in time,
breaks time, breaks words, breaks me, and then,
in silence, leaves me healed and mended.
I leave, returned to language,
for I see through words,
even when all words are ended.
I, who live by words, am wordless,
when I turn me to the Word to pray. Amen

Madeline L'Engle

• • •

Reflecting on the benefits of solitude, stillness, silence and simplicity

- Solitude gives me a sacred place to go to and just to be.

- Solitude is my own fig tree under whose shade I can disengage from all my cares and pressures.

- Solitude allows me to engage with my inner self and the Spirit of God.

• • •

- Stillness quietens all the chatter of my restless mind and spirit.

- Stillness helps me become centred and find my true self.

- Stillness places me in a posture of reception and open to all the free graces of the spiritual world.

• • •

- Silence teaches me to wait – to pray rather than talk, to turn to God first rather than last.

- Silence is said to be the language of God. It is the space between the notes that makes the music. Without that space in between, there is no music, only noise. God comes to me in the silence between the notes.

- In silence I don't have to keep up with outer conversations, so I can pay attention to inner ones and better hear the inner voice of love.

- Silence makes me look and listen, see and smell, to pay attention to what is going on around me, rather than thinking of what next to say, where next to be, what next to do.

- Silence imparts reverence and peacefulness. It is infectious, my tranquillity reaches out and comforts in ways that words cannot.

• • •

- Simplicity is me simply trusting and getting beyond words, ideas and head chatter.

- I can dwell in the 'presence of God' without the need to be talking.

- Being together in 'the Oneness of the Spirit' helps me to see all life as a sacred unified whole and myself as a part of all that is.

- Simplicity is being renewed within and feeling the privilege of just playing my part in the world without striving or fretting.

• • •

A simplified summary

- **Solitude** is to find a place alone yet be in oneness with the Divine Presence and all of life – God in us!

- **Stillness** is to know and sense the Divine Presence in everybody and everything I see, hear, touch, smell and experience – God with us!

- **Silence** is to wait and listen for a gentle word from the Transcendent Presence – God beyond us!

- **Simplicity** is simply to trust and act on the promptings from the 'beyond within' – and know your sacred self – in God!

Concluding Prayers

Awaken me, Lord
To your light.
Open my eyes
To your presence.
Awaken me, Lord
To your love.
Open my heart
To your indwelling.
Awaken me, Lord
To your life.
Open my mind
To your abiding.
Awaken me, Lord
To your purpose.
Open my will
To your guiding.

Teach us, O God, that silent language which says
all things. Teach our souls to remain silent in your
presence; that we might adore you in the depths
of our being and await all things from you, whilst
asking of you nothing but the accomplishment
of your will. Teach us to remain quiet under
your action and produce in our souls that deep
and simple prayer which specifies nothing and
expresses everything. Amen

John Nicholas Grou

Father God, You have told us to listen to your
voice, give us ears to hear your lightest whisper.
The daily work and the rush of life around us,
and the clamour of our own fears and self-
concern, make such a noise that it is difficult to
be quiet before You,
and so we lose the sound of your voice.

Teach us how to shut our doors around us to all
other thoughts and sounds, and to make a deep
silence in our hearts. Then speak to us and we
shall be strong to hear, strong to do,
strong to follow you utterly.
Through Jesus Christ our Lord.

Prayers of Health and Healing

Part Two

Pastoral Helps

We all face times of mental stress, anxiety, fearful thoughts, and even panic attacks. At such times it is helpful to hear and reflect on the words of our faith in order *"to be strong in our inner self,"* as Paul puts it in Ephesians 3:14-21.

If you're like me it's difficult to find solitude and be still and silent. Yet Jesus says,

> when you pray, go into your room, close the door and pray to your Father, who is unseen. Then your Father, who sees what is done in secret, will reward you. (Matthew 6:6).

Jesus said, *"the kingdom of God is within you."* Therefore, it is critical to explore this reality because if we are not in touch with God's Spirit within us, it will be difficult to be in touch with God's Spirit anywhere else!

Underneath all the layers of upbringing, culture, social conditioning, education and ego, we must find our true nature in God – our sacred self, created and loved by God and hidden with Christ in God (refer Colossians 3:3). Before anything else it is vital to know we are a child of God and conceived in love.

Following are 'pastoral helps' that can be drawn on at any time or anywhere. They are simple breathing practices that centre the sacred self, calm the body, and still the mind and soul.

Pastoral Help 1

'Peace be still'

This simple breathing exercise is based on the words of Jesus, **"Peace be still."** He said these words to the disciples when they were in fear of a storm threatening to capsize their boat during a storm. The story records Jesus speaking these words to the waves – but equally they applied to the storm of fear being felt by the disciples and to any storm we might be currently experiencing!

> ***Breathe in*** – *slowly saying 'Peace.'*

> ***Breathe out*** – *slowly saying 'Be still.'*

Repeat for 5 minutes concentrating on hearing your breath and saying the words, ***'Peace – be still.'*** Say the words in your mind or out loud.

Pastoral Help 2

'I have faith & trust'

From Genesis to Revelation, we read many times the words, *"Do not be afraid"* or *"Fear not."* It is one of the most oft repeated phrases in the Bible. Our time on this planet is fleeting, impermanent, we age and wear-out. In consequence we can feel vulnerable and insecure. Offsetting this is the assurance given us in Ecclesiastes, *"that eternity has been set in our hearts."* If we are part of God then we are part of what lives forever! We need to remember we are created and born of God's Spirit and are eternal children of God. *"For you created me and shaped me, gave me life within my mother's womb."* The words of Jesus are instructive when He said, *"In this world you'll have tribulation but be of good cheer I have overcome the world."*

These breathing exercises focus on three selected occasions when *'be not afraid'* assurances are given.

1. "Do not be afraid—I am with you; I am your God—let nothing terrify you! I will make you strong and help you; I will protect you and save you." (Isaiah 41:10), or

   "Be strong and courageous. Do not be frightened, and do not be dismayed, for the Lord your God is with you wherever you go." (Joshua 1:9).

   Breathe in – *'I am not afraid'*
   Breathe out – *'I have faith'*

When Mary received the message that she was to give birth to the promised Messiah she heard the angel say:

"Don't be afraid, Mary. God has been gracious to you. You will become pregnant and give birth to a son, and you call his name Jesus. He will be great and will be called the Son of the Most High God ... The Holy Spirit will come upon you and the power of the Most High will overshadow you."

Breathe in – *'I'm not overwhelmed'*

Breathe out – *'I'm overshadowed'*

2. Jesus, when he was preparing his disciples for his own coming death, said, *"Do not be afraid. Do not be worried or upset. Believe in God and believe in Me."* (John 14:1)

    Breathe in – *'I'm not afraid'*

    Breathe out – *'I believe and trust'*

Pastoral Help 3

'An invitation to come'

Another recurring word in the Scriptures is the word **'Come'** signifying **'invitation.'** The most famous are the words of Jesus in Matthew 11:28 when He invites and calls, *"Come to Me all of you who are tired out from carrying heavy loads."*

By extension He's saying come with all your joys and sorrows, all your failures, doubts, and unbelief. Come with all your questions and concerns, all your anger and hurt, come for acceptance, belonging, healing, hope and renewal. What an invitation!

Christ invites us to 'Himself' not to a system of beliefs or morals or a particular social or cultural way of doing things. Our Christian life is not about the keeping of laws, doctrines and traditions, however helpful they may be, it's about the unconditional and inviting love and grace of God. This reflection is based on four parts of Christ's invitation.

1. **"Come to Me"** – it's a deeply personal invitation to be accepted.
   In my mind I hold the picture of responding and coming into the warm, caring embrace of Christ.

   Breathe in – *'Come to Me' (...insert your name)*

   Breathe out – *'O lamb of God I come'*

2. **"Take my yoke"** – I visualise myself accepting the yoke which has been crafted to fit well and see myself willingly joined to Christ. I remember what Jesus said in John 15 about the vine and branches. *'Remain united to me, and I will remain united to you.'*

   Breathe in – *'I am joined to Christ'*

   Breathe out – *'I am at one with Christ'*

3. **"Learn of Me"** – I see myself sitting down at Christ's feet to learn, even having a notebook to record what Jesus is saying to me or prompting me to think about.

   Breathe in – *'Teach me how to love You'*

   Breathe out – *'Teach me how to pray'*

4. **"and find rest for your soul"** – various translations of John 15 use, *"Dwell or abide in Me and I will dwell or abide in you,"* which suggests I can find complete rest and relaxation by being at home in God's presence

   Breathe in – *'I dwell in God'*

   Breathe out – *'I abide in peace'*

Pastoral Help 4

'A walk in nature'

Breathing exercises can be done with a focus on nature which is a rich source of meditation and contemplation. Take a walk in nature, in a park, along the beach or anywhere that connects you with the flora and fauna and beauty of creation. Allow the experience to engage your senses. Pause to find beauty in unexpected places and reflect on how nature influences you for the good. Sit on a bench and contemplate one bird, one tree or one flower and expand your awareness to see all other birds, trees and flowers. Find a fragrant flower, rose or tree ...

Breathe in – *'I inhale all that is lovely and beautiful.'*

Breathe out – *'I exhale the fragrance and beauty into all I am and do.'*

Windows of Insight

Listen to your life ... touch, taste, smell your way to the holy and hidden heart of it, because in the last analysis all moments are key moments and life itself is grace.

Frederick Buechner

When before the beauty of a sunset or a mountain, you pause and exclaim, 'Ah,' you are participating in divinity.

Ancient Hindu text

All earth is crammed with heaven and every bush aflame with God – but only those who see, take off their shoes.

Elizabeth Browning

If we stop long enough to gaze at what is laid out before us, to let the mystery of beauty and the wonder of the seasons sit deeply in our soul, our hearts cannot help but burst forth in thanksgiving and gratitude to life itself.

Deborah Adele

In the same way, we can train ourselves in what the Chinese called 'quiet sitting' and learn to note the common life that flows through all things, linking them together in harmonious unity. As we sit and watch our natural environment, we should make ourselves aware of the way that birds and leaves, the clouds and the wind, harmonise so that we are not watching a score of different objects but a whole in which each thing has its perfect place. If we develop a mind that 'watches and receives' and discover the fluidity of our natural environment, we may be able to recover some of our ancestors' vision of a sacred nature.

Karen Armstrong

Pastoral Help 5

'The Water of Life'

Reflection

When speaking to the woman Jesus met at the well, there was an amazing discussion about water. Jesus recognised that the woman, indeed all of us, are thirsty for the water of life that truly quenches our thirst for the good and lasting things of life. Remember Jesus said to her:

> Those who drink of this water from the well will
> get thirsty again, but those who drink of the water
> that I will give them will never thirst again. The
> water that I will give them will become in them
> a spring which will provide them with life-giving
> water and give them eternal life. (John 4:1-15).

I visualise coming to the water, thirsty, coming to drink deeply from the river of life, coming to the water, even though weary, coming to rest in the quiet pools of God's love. Coming to be renewed and refreshed in God's ever-flowing stream of grace and love.

Breathe in – *'Dear Lord, give me that water'*

Breathe out – *'I will never thirst again'*

Pastoral Help 6

'The Bread of Life'

Reflection

The second part of this invitation is to focus on the bread that truly satisfies. Isaiah says,

> Why spend money on what is not bread, and your labour on what does not satisfy? Listen, listen to me, and eat what is good, and you will delight in the richest of fare. Give ear and come to me; listen, that you may live. (Isaiah 55:1-2).

Jesus said,

> I am the bread of life, those who come to me will never go hungry; those who believe in me will never be thirsty.

He is our best menu!

Anticipated in these wonderful words is the invitation to come and buy without money from the abundance of God's grace and giving in Jesus Christ. He is the 'Bread of Life' and available in Him is the best possible nourishment for our spiritual life. I will feast on the Bread of Life! I will reflect on the fact that God is here with me, caring for me and feeding me! I need the true bread to sustain me to my journey's end.

Breathe in – *'I receive the Bread of Life'*

Breathe out – *'I am filled and satisfied'*

Pastoral Help 7

'Resting in God'

Reflection

Psalm 23 is one of the most often used portions of scripture, ever! It paints a picture of a 'Shepherd Lord,' leading us to rest in pastures of green grass and beside pools of fresh water, giving us new strength, so that we can be restored and refreshed. The connection to nature is significant and illustrates our connection to the natural environment as places where we can find rest and peace. Notice that it starts with affirmations about God but then moves into a very personal exchange with God about walking through the dark places of life,

> Even if I go through the deepest darkness,
> I will not be afraid, Lord, for you are with me, You,
> are with me and Your rod and staff, comfort me.

A Japanese version of Psalm 23 brings some new insights by using different words:

> The Lord is my Pace-setter, I shall not rush;
> He makes me stop and rest for quiet intervals.
> He provides me with images of stillness, which
> restore my serenity;
> He leads me in ways of efficiency through calmness
> of mind, and His guidance is peace. Even though I
> have a great many things to accomplish each day,
> I will not fret, for His presence is here.
> His timelessness, His all-importance, will keep me
> in balance.

He prepares refreshment and renewal in the midst of my activity, anointing my mind with His oils of tranquillity. My cup of joyous energy overflows. Surely harmony and effectiveness shall be the fruits of my hours,
For I shall walk in the pace of my Lord, and dwell in His house forever.

Breathe in – *'I rest in God'*

Breathe out – *'I am refreshed in God'*

Pastoral Help 8

'Be still in God'

This exercise is based on the well-known verse from Psalm 46; *"Be still and know that I am God."* What we will do is progressively drop the last word off each portion of the verse remaining. Do this practice very slowly allowing 20 minutes. Using the words in bold, breathe in and out repeating five times.

"Be still and know that I am God"

I consciously move from thinking about myself to contemplating God. This is about orientating my focus. This affirmation takes me beyond myself to the 'divine other' – the source and sustainer of all life.

I consciously move from my false-self or little-self to my true-self, from my separate-self to my connected-self, from my ego-self to my Christ centred-self, from being two to being joined in 'oneness' with God's Spirit. This coming together of the human and the divine is what Jesus revealed in his incarnation.

"Be still and know that I am"

I affirm that I am, that I am a conscious creation and part of God. That I belong to God from whom I came. Then call to mind the seven **'I am'** sayings that St John described Jesus as being. Spend time with each affirmation letting it lead your mind and spirit to explore what each 'I am' statement means for you. Acknowledge that the 'Great I am' loves me as a part of creation and therefore I am of great worth and value. I rest my personal 'I am' in the grace and creative purposes of God – causing a deep gratitude for all aspects of my life and for the amazing experience of life itself.

> I am the bread of life
> I am the light of the world
> I am the door
> I am the good shepherd
> I am the resurrection and the life
> I am the way, the truth and the life
> I am the true vine.

"Be still and know"

I will concentrate on knowing the life, ways and teachings of Jesus deep within my heart. Having a deep spiritual knowing, is *"to have the mind of Christ within me,"* as St Paul put it. Being in Christ is to move from the limitations of my 'little story' to know and be part of the 'big story' of God which is exciting!

Use the Beatitudes of Jesus in Matthew 5, I further expand my focus on his teachings...

> Happy are those who know they are
> spiritually poor;
> the Kingdom of heaven belongs to them!

> Happy are those who mourn;
> God will comfort them!

> Happy are those who are humble;
> they will receive what God has promised!

> Happy are those whose greatest desire
> is to do what God requires;
> God will satisfy them fully!

> Happy are those who are merciful to others,
> God will be merciful to them!

Happy are the pure in heart;
they will see God!

Happy are those who work for peace;
God will call them his children!

Happy are those who are persecuted because
they do what God requires
...the Kingdom of Heaven belongs to them!

"Be still"

I consciously will 'be still' in body, mind and spirit, doing so in solitude, stillness and silence. Applying myself to prayer, meditation and contemplation develops my interior spirituality and purifies my intent and influences my exterior behaviour and actions, and my service and love of others.

"Be"

I will relax and have a sense of dwelling in the presence of God and living completely in the moment. I reflect on how Jesus used the concept of 'abiding' in the vine, (John 15:1-5). So much of my living is about busyness but this is my opportunity to focus on resting and abiding in the vine of God's grace and also knowing that I'm connected to all things in God! This realignment of 'myself' from 'individualism' to 'oneness' becomes the very essence of my heart, open to God's transforming Spirit and indwelling Presence.

Additional Notes:

The above are only suggestions so feel free to develop your own understandings and descriptions around these steps. The more personal you can make these exercises in prayer and meditation the better.

Pastoral Help 9

'Divine abidings'

We can learn a great deal by being open to the teachings of great religious and spiritual figures from other times and faiths. In the Buddhist tradition there are many suggestions on how to move beyond our human limitations to engage with the wider and spiritual world. Faced with the enormity of the challenges before humankind and the survival of the planet we can easily give up, feeling powerless and hopeless. However, we can still make a meaningful contribution if we take on board what Alfred Lord Tennyson said, *"More change is wrought by prayer than this world dreams of."* Here is something we can all do! Hope is said to be, *"the joyful anticipation of all things good."* We can actively encourage this realisation through our meditations and prayers. The following affirmations will help you exert influence on world affairs which is an enormous claim to make, yet in the spiritual realm as Jesus said, *"with God all things are possible."*

The four divine abidings & meditations

- **Love kindness** – I engage myself in longing for the benefit and welfare of all beings, including enemies.

- **Compassion** – I actively reflect on all people and situations of distress, sorrow and suffering.

- **Joyful affirming** – I identify causes for rejoicing and affirm the prosperity and successes of others.

- **Serenity** – I see myself rising above anger and hate, tyranny and oppression, wealth and want and regard my own life and circumstance with impartial calmness and tranquillity.

Breathe in – *'I share loving kindness'*

Breathe out – *'I long for the welfare of all'*

Breathe in – *'I have compassion for all living things'*

Breathe out – *'I accept the sorrows and sufferings of life'*

Breathe in – *'I joyfully affirm all that is good'*

Breathe out – *'I want peace and prosperity for all'*

Breathe in – *'I'll work for peace and justice for all'*

Breathe out – *'I affirm and enjoy oneness with God'*

Pastoral Help 10

'Belonging in Oneness'

Reflection

Jesus spoke and prayed often that we would be at one with God and each other. Indeed, the very word 'atonement' means being made one with God, 'at-one-with.' Jesus knew the true nature of what God had created when the universe came into existence, and it was that everything is part of the whole. Today, the new science of quantum physics reveals that all things are part of that whole. Everything belongs and is deeply connected and in relationship. We are all one piece! You will have heard of the 'butterfly effect' which simply suggests that even the flapping of a butterfly's delicate wing is enough to create an ongoing effect that reaches the other side of the world. It's the idea that the flap of a butterfly's wing in New Zealand could hypothetically cause a weather disturbance in Australia – incredible as it may seem! As Einstein said, *"what we have called matter is energy; matter is spirit reduced to the point of visibility. There is no matter."* All life and matter are forms of interconnected energy. Eco-science is also revealing just how interconnected everything is and climate change is a negative proof of this. Jesus invites us to reflect on nature (Matthew 6) and ponder its beauty and how without toil or effort, it just is! We can look through nature's windows to view the remarkableness of the world we are inextricably connected to. The ethic of Jesus demonstrated how everything, and everybody is in relationship and that we all have an effect for good or ill on nature and each other. This is why He stressed the importance of forgiveness, even of our enemies. To do so is to not only to encourage restoration of the person but is in our own best interests because the common good is better served. Unforgiveness and exclusion is always a continuing source of division and trouble.

We like to think we are separate autonomous individuals, but we are not. The sin of Adam and Eve referred to in the book of Genesis was the selfish decision that they wanted to do things their own way with consequent separation from relationship with God and others, and the loss of the joy of togetherness which God intended. The truth is that *"we live and move and have our being"* in relationship to the world, all nations, peoples, and each other. Oneness is a divine principle of life – it is the fundamental design of life. One light, many colours; one water, many thirsts; one essence, many shapes and forms. To function properly our bodies must function as one. We are encouraged to see all people as brothers and sisters and as part of the family of God. St Paul used the analogy of the body of Christ with each person being an essential member of the body of God.

A practice to affirm Belonging and Oneness:

- I reflect on the words of Jesus when He said, *"I pray that they may all be one, Father. May they be in us just as you are in me, and I am in you."*

- I reflect on the words of St Paul, *"There is one Lord, one faith, one baptism, there is one God and Father of all humankind who is Lord of all, works through all, and is in all."* (Ephesians 4:4-5)

- I see myself as a member of the Body of Christ. (John.15; 1 Corinthians 12: 12)

- I visualise myself in a large crowd and without judgement see everyone as children of God and myself as part of this rich, diverse family of God.

- I feel the energy of creation connecting me to nature and all living things.

Windows of Insight

The understanding that I am a holy child of God contains within itself often unrealized consequences. If I embrace this notion about myself, I must accept its corollary: that is, if I am a holy child of God, then so is everyone else. "Oneness is an easy thing to profess, until we realise that it must include not only the people we like and agree with, not only those to whom we are sympathetic, but also those whom we view as abhorrent (whatever side of a political position we may hold). We don't get to choose who we are one with—it's everybody.

Howard Thurman points to the centrality of the love ethic in Jesus's teachings. He observes the types of people Jesus befriended who, by all accounts, should have been absolute enemies. Thurman points to the necessity of extinguishing bitterness within the heart in order to recognize adversaries as holy children of God.

Howard Thurman & Father Richard Rohr

We are tied together in the single garment of destiny, caught in an inescapable network of mutuality. And whatever affects one directly affects all indirectly.

Martin Luther King. Jr.

Gratitude celebrates life with a joyful **'Yes'** at every knot of the great network in which everything is connected to everything.

Br. David Steindl-Rast

Every being exists in intimate relation with other beings and in constant exchange of gifts with each other. But this relationship is beyond pragmatic use. It is rather a mutual sharing of existence in the grand venture of the universe itself.

Thomas Berry

There is an endless net of threads throughout the universe. The horizontal threads are in space. The vertical threads are in time. At every crossing of the threads, there is an individual, and every individual is a crystal bead. And every crystal bead reflects not only the light from every other crystal in the net, but also every other reflection throughout the entire universe.

Rig Veda

Jesus himself was archetypally hung between a good thief and a bad thief, between heaven and earth, holding together both his humanity and his divinity, a male body with a feminine soul. He was a Jewish believer who forgave and loved everyone else. Christ "reconciled all things in himself" (Ephesians 2:14-16). Jesus really is an icon of what Carl Jung called the holy and whole-making spirit ...

Jesus did not come to found a separate or new religion as much as he came to present a universal message of vulnerability and foundational unity that is necessary for all religions, the human soul, and history itself to survive. Thus, Christians can rightly call Jesus "the Saviour of the world" (John 4:42), but no longer in the competitive and imperialistic way that they have usually presented him. By very definition, vulnerability and unity do not compete or dominate. The cosmic Christ is no threat to anything but separateness, illusion, domination, and the imperial ego.

Father Richard Rohr

To be alive in this beautiful, self-organising universe – to participate in the dance of life with senses to perceive it, lungs that breathe it, organs that draw nourishment from it – is a wonder beyond words.

Joanna Macy

Through me course wide rivers and in me rise tall mountains. And beyond the thickets of my agitation and confusion there stretch the wide plains of my peace and surrender. All landscapes are within me. And there is room for everything.

Etty Hillesum

It Is Difficult, O God It is difficult,
O God it was much easier
before we lived in our own world
we took that world for the entire world,
we believed we were your chosen people,
with special privileges and advantages
we thought we had nothing to learn from people,
who were different from us
in what they believed,
and how they lived but suddenly
all these people are all over the place,
they come to live in our midst
they speak all sorts of languages,
they practise different faiths,
they even dress differently.

It is complicated, O God
it was much simpler in the past
we lived among like-minded people

we used to understand each other,
we ate the same food
we shared the common thoughts,
we even acquired the same habits,
we seldom ventured out of our compound,
we were contented with what we knew,
but all of a sudden,
the walls that separated us
from other people crumbled
we have lost control of our life.
We are afraid we are no longer masters
of our own destiny.

But it has never been easy for you,
O God it has never been simple for You.
You, have always dealt with a world of
wonderful plurality,
with many people and many nations
with many cultures and religions,
with women as well as men with children
as well men and women.
But instead of complaining, You enjoy it,
instead of becoming upset, You delight in it.
Though it is still difficult for us help us,
O God, to enjoy it with all its multiplicity,
though it is still too complicated for us,
enable us,
O God, to cope with it
with the spirit of gratitude and wonder
and inspire us to know ever more deeply
the mystery that is
Yours the truth, You alone can disclose to us.

Choan-Seng Song
Professor Emeritus of Theology and Asian Cultures

Pastoral Help 11

'Interactive Scripture reading'

Reflection

Reading the Bible or any significant literature with just our mind engaged is a very inadequate way to do so. Like Nathaniel, once under the fig tree or in our place of solitude and stillness, we can engage in the **'reflective reading'** of a selected passage. To plumb the depths of meaning requires the use of our imagination and spiritual understanding rather than just our critical mind. Then our reading moves beyond just an academic exercise to one of spiritual discernment. As an old hymn says, *"Beyond the sacred page I seek thee Lord."* Rather than reading scripture we ought to **'reflect on and study scripture'** because we go beyond the surface and literal meaning to the inner and deeper spiritual and eternal truths. To gain the most from our reflection on scripture we need to be interactive with it. Below are three examples of how we can do this:

The method of meditation using 'reflective reading'

- Select a scripture passage. Read carefully and attentively. Read several times – perhaps out loud – absorb it.

- Now think deeply, uncover the depths of what you've read, a little bit like 'chewing the cud.' This becomes an exercise of our inner understanding.

- Allow your heart to respond through prayer. It is said that we speak to God in prayer and God speaks to us through the words of scripture. You may identify yourself in the actions or words of one of the people in the scripture passage or story. You may be reminded of an area of your life that needs attention. Here you bring your heart and mind to God. This is a response of desire and intention which will be rewarded.

- A simple resting in God or contemplation. This is the imageless prayer that goes beyond all sense and thought to a simple being in the presence of God.

- This contemplation, or resting in God, is seen as a gift, and a natural progression from pondering deeply the written word of God, to a place of listening deeply and resting in the living word of God, comprehended in our own heart and mind.

Example 1: 'Choosing the better part'

Remember the story of Mary & Martha from Luke 10:41-42. *"Martha was upset about all the work she had to do ... but Mary has chosen the better part, and it shall not be taken away from her."* And what was Mary doing? Mary was simply sitting at the feet of the Lord attentively listening. This is exactly what we do in prayer and meditation. Martha was probably busy getting lunch. Biblical commentators point out that if she hadn't been, then perhaps the three of them would have gone hungry that day. But the point here is that there is a time for prayer and a time for getting lunch. I'm sure Mary would have helped with housework afterwards.

This is a reminder that we have within us both a contemplative and active posture. There is no such person as a 'contemplative' alone, while others are just 'actives.' We are all to combine the call to prayer and the call to fruitful action in our lives. But let us not forget that Jesus did say that Mary on that occasion had chosen the better part! Listening and reflecting comes before action and doing.

A practice on 'choosing the better part':

- I position myself comfortably.

- I see myself like Mary sitting at the feet of Jesus.

- Listen for the word Christ wants to speak to me.

- Record what I heard and/or felt.

Example 2: 'Coping with the fevers of life'

This incident in Mark 1:29-34 was a private miracle and is the story about the fevers of life. Jesus didn't need a big crowd. It was not a performance for the benefit of bringing attention to himself. There was no publicity; there was no crowd to be impressed. All too often we're at our best in public and our worst at home – not so Jesus, he is a picture of a balanced life. Here is a simple cottage scene and a woman with a fever. The story records that Peter's mother-in-law had a fever. We too have our fevers. Life can get on top of us. Overwork, worry, anxiety, depression, fatigue, stress related illnesses, emptiness, meaninglessness, all suggesting a life out of balance and not centred.

A practice to cope with the fevers of life:

- Reflect on the actions of Jesus.

- **'He went to her'** – He comes to me!

- **'Took her hand'** – I feel His touch, reassurance, tenderness and caring.

- **'He raised her up'** – I receive and feel the flow of His energy and power, lifting me up and helping me cope.

- **'The fever left her'** – calmed in my mind and spirit, I now feel restored to a normal balanced life.

- **'She attended to their needs'** – what might I be restored to do?

- In time apart with God, reflecting on my life and gifts, taking some deep breaths I tap into the ultimate resources of restoration. I am raised up to share God's love and power and to serve in new ways. I am made strong for service, *"I will raise you up on eagle's wings."*

- Restored through prayer, reflection, and faith I can reach out to share the good news. I can be part of that good news!

- Healing is the transfer of Jesus' power and life into mine. He shares his life with me. New hope is given. A new reason and purpose for living is found.

Example 3: 'On board with Jesus'

The sea is a very good metaphor for faith. It is ceaselessly changing, never still, never fixed, has no permanent form or shape. As a metaphor for faith, it is in marked contrast to fixed beliefs set out in neat doctrinal statements. Traditional religion can become dogma and is unwilling to change. Such is our need for certainty that we make an idol of what we believe and miss the whole point of living by faith. We can end up with a fixed mind. One that is shut fast to new truth. We base what we believe on other people's experience who lived in bygone ages. Such fixed belief and certainty become a denial of the reality of life because if nothing else life is not certain, it is incredibly uncertain and changeable. The gospel story of Jesus calming the sea is rich in symbolism. It is a combination of 'history remembered' and important spiritual truth being expressed.

Storms came up suddenly on the Sea of Galilee. Our storms can be sudden too, a domestic storm, loss of employment, a relationship storm, financial or a storm of illness. News of a sudden death can come in one phone call. The bad news from a doctor of a terminal illness. Suddenly, the whole of life is turned upside down.

Notice, just because Jesus is in the boat, doesn't mean there are no storms. Many Christians wrongly think Christian faith protects us from storms and that storms are judgements on the ungodly. You can be in the very centre of God's will yet be going through a hurricane of some kind. In fact, if you follow Jesus and his teachings, you are much more likely to facing storms than if you seek the comfort and security of the world. The rain falls on the good and the bad, Jesus said; storms happen to us all. Storms are the stuff of life, no one is exempt, but they can be a way to find God's Spirit and Presence in the storms and circumstances of our life to give us courage and make us stronger. Of course, it makes all the difference in the world who you have with you in your boat during the storm!

A practice of 'being on-board with Jesus.'

(Mark 4:35-41; Luke 8:22-25)

- I name some of the storms I've come through.

- What were my feelings and how did I cope?

- Was I aware of the protecting presence of Christ on board?

- In the storms of life do I hear Jesus addressing the waves and stilling the storms that threaten my inner life and peace.

- I listen for the words of Christ, 'Peace be still.'

- I hear the words of Jesus saying, 'let us go to the other side.'

- I am invited to view life from God's side and appreciate the alternative vision and understanding of life revealed in Christ.

- I sense a new direction and purpose emerging.

- I learn of Christ's mastery. I know his peace.

- I hear his words addressed to me, 'Peace, be still', in all the turbulent circumstances of my life and discover his power to overcome and give inner peace and calm.

- "Who is it that can make muddy water clear? No one. But left to stand, it will gradually clear itself." *Lao Tzu*

In the words of an ancient prayer...

> O God of peace, who has taught us that in returning and rest we shall be saved, that in quietness and confidence shall be our strength; by the might of your spirit lift us to yourself, to your presence where we might be still and know that you are God.

Windows of insight

> Reading the scriptures is not as easy as it seems. We tend to make everything subject to analysis and discussion since in our academic world we tend to make anything and everything subject to analysis and discussion. But the Word of God should lead us first of all to contemplation and meditation. Instead of taking the words apart, we should bring them together in our inmost being. Instead of wondering if we agree or disagree, we should identify which words are directly spoken to us and connect directly to our personal story. Instead of thinking about the words as potential subjects for an interesting dialogue (or sermon) we should be willing to let those words penetrate the most hidden corners of our heart, even to those places where no other word has yet found entrance. Then and only then can the 'living word' bear fruit like

seed sown in rich soil. Only then can we really 'hear and understand.' (Matthew 12:23)

Contemplative and reflective reading of scripture draws us into silence; silence makes us attentive to God's Word. The Word of God penetrates through the thick verbosity to the silent centre of our heart; silence opens us up to the space where the word can be heard. Without reading the word, silence becomes stale, and without silence, the word loses its re-creative power. The word leads to silence and silence to the word. The word is born in silence, and silence is the deepest response to the word.

Henri Nouwen

Because this Word is a hidden Word
It comes in the darkness of the night.
To enter this darkness put away,
all voices and sounds
all images and likenesses.
In stillness and peace
in this unknowing knowledge
God speaks to the soul
and becomes fully expressed there.

Meister Eckhart

Concluding comment

The whole aim of meditation and this booklet is to encourage an intimate and loving relationship with the Divine Presence.

Teresa of Ávila said *"One finds God in oneself, and one finds oneself in God."* Both are wonderfully true!

The mystic Mechthild of Magdeburg (c.1207–c.1282) wrote about her experience and records a conversation between her soul and God's Spirit:

The soul begins:

Ah, Lord, love me passionately, love me often,
love me long. For the more continuously You love
me, the purer I will be; the more fervently You
love me, the more beautiful I will be;
the longer You love me,
the holier I will become here on earth.

God responds:

Because I Myself am Love,
I will love you continuously.
Because I long to be loved passionately,
my desire is to love you fervently.
Because I am everlasting and eternal,
I will love you long...
When I shine, you will reflect my radiance,
When I flow, you will flow swiftly,
When you breathe, you draw into yourself
My Divine Heart.
When you cry for Me, I take you into My arms.
When you love Me, we are united as one.
Nothing can separate us,
for we abide together joyfully.
He brought me to his banqueting table
and his banner over me is love.
My beloved belongs to me, and I am his;
he pastures his flock among the lilies.

Songs of Solomon 2: 4 & 16

Pastoral Help 12

'A meditation using music'

Most people appreciate music in its various genres. It would be hard to imagine life without music! Music is everywhere. Nature gives us bird song and the sounds of the elements. Science tells us that even the stars have musical sounds and literature references the 'music of the spheres,' even as the dolphins and whales of the deep generate their own sounds.

Music is based on harmony, (think of an orchestra), and can be very beneficial in drawing us into its own harmonies and making possible a deep sense of inner harmony in ourselves. Interestingly, for there to be music there must be spaces between the notes!

We all have our favourite pieces of music, which we can use to nourish our minds and hearts by doing this practical meditation:

A meditation in music

- Select a piece of uplifting music and play it on repeat. Let the music transport you to other places, then bring you back to hear it deep within yourself.

- Imagine the music taking away all discord and dis-harmony in you and around you.

- Let the music wash over you, inviting its harmonies to enter your inner life, resonating deep within you, creating harmony and oneness.

- If the music has lyrics quietly sing, say, or reflect on the words absorbing their meaning into the deep recesses of your being.

- Quietly sit with the music and appreciate the 'spaces between the notes.' What message is the music conveying to you?

My favourite pieces of music for meditation are excerpts from Handel's *Messiah*. For me they help to confirm my faith and hope in a loving, inviting God who we best understand in the coming of Jesus Christ, *"For unto us a Child is born...,"* as the oratorio puts it. Handel's *Messiah* brings together wonderful music and words encompassing the advent of Christ, his death and resurrection and marvellously climaxes in the Hallelujah Chorus!

> He shall feed His flock like a shepherd,
> and He shall gather the lambs with His arm,
> and carry them in His bosom,
> and gently lead those that are with young.
>
> *Isaiah 40:11 (No. 20 – Air)*

> Come unto Him, all ye that labour,
> come unto Him ye that are heavy laden,
> and He will give you rest.
>
> Take His yoke upon you, and learn of Him,
> for He is meek and lowly of heart,
> and ye shall find rest unto your souls.
>
> *Matthew 11:28–29 (No. 20 – Air)*

> How beautiful are the feet of them
> that preach the gospel of peace
> and bring glad tidings of good things!
>
> *Isaiah 52:7; Romans 10:15 (No. 38 – Air)*

Benediction

Lord, it is night.

The night is for stillness.
Let us be still in the presence of God.

It is night after a long day.
What has been done has been done;
what has not been done has not been done;
let it be.

The night is dark.
Let our fears of the darkness of the world
and of our own lives
rest in you.

The night is quiet.
Let the quietness of your peace enfold us,
all dear to us,
and all who have no peace.

The night heralds the dawn.
Let us look expectantly to a new day,
new joys,
new possibilities.

In your name we pray.
Amen.

'Night Prayer' from A New Zealand Prayer Book,
He Karakia Mihinare o Aotearoa
by Rev. John Williamson

Also by Ian M Kilgour

The Art of Dying Well:
Ideas and reflections to help you face your death with courage, peace and hope

By Ian M Kilgour

Published: 2019
B/W text, 80pp, 6″ x 9″
Soft cover
ISBN: 9781988572048

This book will help you face your own death with courage and faith. Some simple things can help ease your mind and bring peace to your heart.

Much of the book is written in the first-person singular to help you personalise your reflections.

There are many prompts for you to write in a notebook or journal your reflections and memories of significant people, places and events in your life, and ideas for your funeral.

Dip into the book where and when you want, pondering only one or two paragraphs at a time. It includes readings and meditations from a wide range of perspectives and faith traditions.

Print books and eBook editions available at
www.philipgarsidebooks.com

www.ingramcontent.com/pod-product-compliance
Lightning Source LLC
Chambersburg PA
CBHW031232120626
46545CB00003B/1095